DBT Workbook for Neurc

Tailored Techniques for Autism, ADHD, Special Needs, and Beyond

Alberta Osborn James

Unlock the power of Dialectical Behaviour Therapy specifically tailored for neurodivergent individuals! Dive into the "DBT Workbook for Neurodivergent Individuals: Tailored Techniques for Autism, ADHD, Special Needs, and Beyond" and discover a world of empowering strategies, practical exercises, and life-changing insights. Are you ready to transform your emotional resilience and embrace your unique strengths? Stay tuned for the big reveal!

Contents

Chapter 1: Introduction

Dialectical Behavioural Therapy (DBT) is a type of cognitive-behavioural therapy that was developed by Marsha M. Linehan in the late 1980s as a treatment for borderline personality disorder. Over the years, DBT has been found to be effective for treating a variety of mental health conditions, including depression, anxiety, post-traumatic stress disorder, and substance use disorders. In recent years, there has been growing interest in using DBT to treat individuals with neurodivergent conditions such as autism spectrum disorder, ADHD, dyslexia, and Tourette syndrome.

DBT is a skills-based therapy that is typically delivered in a group format over the course of several months. The therapy is designed to help individuals learn skills to manage their emotions, regulate their behavior, and improve their interpersonal relationships. The therapy is grounded in four key modules: mindfulness, distress tolerance, emotion regulation, and interpersonal effectiveness.

Mindfulness: Mindfulness is the first module of DBT and involves paying attention to the present moment without judgment. For individuals with neurodivergent conditions, mindfulness can be particularly helpful because it can help them to regulate their emotions and reduce their anxiety. Practicing mindfulness can also help individuals with neurodivergent conditions to become more aware of their body sensations, which can be an important tool for managing sensory overload.

Distress Tolerance: The second module of DBT is distress tolerance, which involves learning skills to cope with distressing situations without making the situation worse. For individuals with neurodivergent conditions, distress tolerance can be particularly important because they may experience heightened emotional reactions to stressors in their environment. Learning skills to cope with distressing situations can help these individuals to manage their emotions more effectively and prevent them from becoming overwhelmed.

Emotion Regulation: The third module of DBT is emotion regulation, which involves learning skills to identify and manage emotions. For individuals with neurodivergent conditions, emotion regulation can be particularly important because they may experience difficulty identifying and labeling their emotions. Learning skills to regulate their emotions can help these individuals to improve their emotional stability and reduce mood swings.

Interpersonal Effectiveness: The fourth and final module of DBT is interpersonal effectiveness, which involves learning skills to improve communication and build healthy relationships with others. For individuals with neurodivergent conditions, interpersonal effectiveness can be particularly important because they may struggle with social skills and building meaningful connections with others. Learning skills to improve communication and build healthy relationships can help these individuals to improve their quality of life and reduce feelings of isolation.

Benefits of DBT for Neurodivergent Individuals: DBT can offer several benefits for individuals with neurodivergent conditions, including:

1. Improved emotion regulation: DBT can help individuals with neurodivergent conditions to improve their emotional stability and reduce mood swings. By learning skills to identify and regulate their emotions, these individuals can better manage their reactions to stressors in their environment.

2. Increased distress tolerance: DBT can help individuals with neurodivergent conditions to develop skills to cope with distressing situations without making the situation worse. By learning skills to tolerate distress, these individuals can better manage their emotional reactions to stressors in their environment.

3. Improved communication and relationships: DBT can help individuals with neurodivergent conditions to improve their social skills and build healthy relationships with others. By learning skills to improve communication and build healthy relationships, these individuals can reduce feelings of isolation and improve their quality of life.

4. Enhanced self-awareness: DBT can help individuals with neurodivergent conditions to become more self-aware by learning mindfulness skills. By paying attention to the present moment without judgment, individuals can become more aware of their body sensations, emotions, and thoughts. This increased self-awareness can help these individuals to manage their emotions and behaviour more effectively and improve their overall well-being.

5. Adaptability and customization: DBT is a highly adaptable therapy that can be customized to meet the unique needs of each individual. This is particularly important for individuals with neurodivergent conditions, who may have different challenges and strengths when it comes to managing their emotions and behaviour. By customizing DBT to meet the needs of each individual, therapists can help these individuals to achieve the best possible outcomes from therapy.

6. Accessible and supportive: DBT can be delivered in a group format, which can provide a supportive and non-judgmental environment for individuals with neurodivergent conditions. Group therapy can provide a sense of community and belonging, which can be particularly important for individuals who may struggle with social skills and building meaningful connections with others.

7. Skills-based approach: DBT is a skills-based therapy, which means that individuals are taught specific skills to manage their emotions and behaviour. This can be particularly helpful for individuals with neurodivergent conditions, who may benefit from a structured approach to therapy that focuses on building specific skills and strategies.

8. Challenges of DBT for Neurodivergent Individuals: While DBT can offer many benefits for individuals with neurodivergent conditions, there are also some challenges to consider, including:

9. Learning new skills: Learning new skills can be challenging for individuals with neurodivergent conditions, who may struggle with executive functioning, attention, and memory. It may take longer for these individuals to learn and integrate new skills into their daily lives.

10. Sensory overload: For individuals with sensory processing difficulties, the group therapy format of DBT may be overwhelming. Therapists may need to make adjustments to the therapy environment to accommodate these individuals.

11. Customization: While DBT can be customized to meet the unique needs of each individual, it can be challenging to find the right balance between providing structure and flexibility in therapy. Therapists may need to adjust their approach to

therapy based on the needs and preferences of each individual.

12. Adapting skills: Some of the skills taught in DBT may need to be adapted for individuals with neurodivergent conditions. For example, mindfulness exercises may need to be adapted to accommodate sensory processing difficulties.

Dialectical Behavioural Therapy (DBT) is a skills-based therapy that can be highly beneficial for individuals with neurodivergent conditions. By learning skills to manage their emotions, regulate their behaviour, and improve their interpersonal relationships, individuals with neurodivergent conditions can improve their overall well-being and quality of life. While there are some challenges to consider when adapting DBT for neurodivergent individuals, the benefits of this therapy can be significant and life-changing. It is important for therapists and individuals to work together to customize DBT to meet the unique needs of each individual and achieve the best possible outcomes from therapy.

Neurodivergent-friendly approach to DBT

The neurodivergent-friendly approach to DBT involves adapting the therapy to meet the unique needs of individuals with neurodivergent conditions. This approach recognizes that individuals with neurodivergent conditions may have different challenges and strengths when it comes to managing their emotions and behavior, and that traditional DBT may not be fully effective for these individuals without some modifications.

The neurodivergent-friendly approach to DBT involves several key principles, including:

1. Individualized treatment plans: Therapists who take a neurodivergent-friendly approach to DBT will work with each individual to develop a treatment plan that is tailored to their specific needs and preferences. This may involve customizing the therapy modules, adapting skills and strategies, and providing additional support as needed.

2. Sensory accommodations: Individuals with neurodivergent conditions may have sensory processing difficulties, and the group therapy format of DBT may be overwhelming for some individuals. Therapists who take a neurodivergent-friendly approach may make adjustments to the therapy environment to accommodate these individuals, such as using sensory-friendly lighting, providing noise-cancelling headphones, or allowing breaks as needed.

3. Flexibility and creativity: Therapists who take a neurodivergent-friendly approach may need to be more flexible and creative in their approach to therapy. This may involve using visual aids,

providing additional explanations or examples, or adapting skills and strategies to meet the unique needs of each individual.

4. Emphasizing strengths: Therapists who take a neurodivergent-friendly approach may also focus on the strengths of each individual, rather than just their challenges. This can help individuals to build confidence and motivation, and to see themselves as capable and valuable members of their communities.

Some examples of how DBT can be adapted for individuals with neurodivergent conditions include:

1. Using visual aids: For individuals with dyslexia or other learning disabilities, visual aids can be helpful in learning new skills and strategies. Therapists may use diagrams, charts, or other visual aids to help explain concepts and skills.

2. Providing additional examples: Individuals with autism spectrum disorder or other conditions that affect social skills may benefit from additional examples of how to use interpersonal effectiveness skills in real-life situations. Therapists may provide examples of specific social situations and how to use skills to navigate those situations.

3. Adapting mindfulness exercises: For individuals with sensory processing difficulties, traditional mindfulness exercises may be overwhelming.

Therapists may adapt mindfulness exercises to accommodate these individuals, such as using breathing exercises that involve counting or visualizations.

4. Focusing on strengths: Individuals with neurodivergent conditions may benefit from a strengths-based approach to therapy. Therapists may focus on the individual's strengths and accomplishments, rather than just their challenges, to build motivation and self-esteem.

Case Study 1: Sarah

Sarah is a 24-year-old woman with ADHD and anxiety. She struggles with regulating her emotions and often experiences intense mood swings. Sarah finds it difficult to concentrate during therapy sessions and frequently interrupts others. The therapist adapts the mindfulness module by providing Sarah with visual aids, such as diagrams and videos, to help her focus during mindfulness exercises. The therapist also works with Sarah to develop strategies for managing her impulsivity during group sessions, such as using a fidget toy or taking breaks when needed.

Case Study 2: David

David is a 16-year-old boy with autism spectrum disorder. He struggles with social skills and often feels isolated from his peers. David finds it difficult to understand and use interpersonal effectiveness skills in real-life situations. The therapist adapts the interpersonal effectiveness module by providing David with additional examples of social situations and role-playing exercises to help him practice using skills in a safe environment. The therapist also works with David to identify his strengths and interests and encourages him to explore activities that align with those strengths.

Case Study 3: Emma

Emma is a 32-year-old woman with dyslexia and depression. She struggles with regulating her emotions and often feels overwhelmed by her feelings. Emma finds it difficult to follow along during therapy sessions and frequently forgets the skills she has learned. The therapist adapts the emotion regulation module by providing Emma with visual aids, such as flowcharts and diagrams, to help her understand and remember the skills she has learned. The therapist also works with Emma to develop strategies for managing her emotions outside of therapy, such as using a mood tracker or journaling.

Case Study 4: Alex

Alex is a 19-year-old non-binary individual with Tourette syndrome and anxiety. They struggle with regulating their emotions and often feel overwhelmed by their tics. Alex finds it difficult to participate in group therapy sessions because they feel self-conscious about their tics. The therapist adapts the distress tolerance module by providing Alex with sensory accommodations, such as noise-cancelling headphones or a weighted blanket, to help them feel more comfortable during therapy sessions. The therapist also works with Alex to develop strategies for managing their anxiety and reducing their self-consciousness during group therapy.

Case Study 5: Javier

Javier is a 28-year-old man with ADHD and substance use disorder. He struggles with regulating his emotions and often experiences intense mood swings. Javier finds it difficult to concentrate during therapy sessions and frequently interrupts others. The therapist adapts the emotion regulation module by providing Javier with visual aids, such as diagrams and videos, to help him understand the skills he has learned. The therapist also works with Javier to develop strategies for managing his impulsivity and avoiding triggers for substance use.

Case Study 6: Leah

Leah is a 23-year-old woman with autism spectrum disorder and depression. She struggles with regulating her emotions and often feels overwhelmed by her feelings. Leah finds it difficult to participate in group therapy sessions because she feels anxious around others. The therapist adapts the distress tolerance module by providing Leah with individual therapy sessions and incorporating sensory accommodations, such as dim lighting and calming music, into the therapy environment. The therapist also works with Leah to develop strategies for managing her anxiety and building social skills outside of therapy.

Case Study 7: Tom

Tom is a 30-year-old man with dyslexia and bipolar disorder. He struggles with regulating his emotions and often experiences intense mood swings. Tom finds it difficult to follow along during therapy sessions and frequently forgets the skills he has learned. The therapist adapts the emotion regulation module by providing Tom with visual aids, such as charts and diagrams, to help him understand and remember the skills he has learned. The therapist also works with Tom to develop strategies for managing his bipolar disorder, such as using a mood tracker and setting realistic goals for himself.

Case Study 8: Sophie

Sophie is a 20-year-old woman with ADHD and anxiety. She struggles with regulating her emotions and often feels overwhelmed by her feelings. Sophie finds it difficult to participate in group therapy sessions because she feels anxious around others. The therapist adapts the distress tolerance module by providing Sophie with individual therapy sessions and incorporating sensory accommodations, such as a calming scent and a comfortable chair, into the therapy environment. The therapist also works with Sophie to develop strategies for managing her anxiety and building social skills outside of therapy.

Case Study 9: Jake

Jake is a 18-year-old boy with Tourette syndrome and anxiety. He struggles with regulating his emotions and often feels overwhelmed by his tics. Jake finds it difficult to follow along during therapy sessions and frequently forgets the skills he has learned. The therapist adapts the mindfulness module by providing Jake with visual aids, such as breathing exercises and progressive muscle relaxation techniques, to help him regulate his tics and focus during therapy sessions. The therapist also works with Jake to develop strategies for managing his anxiety and reducing his self-consciousness during group therapy.

Case Study 10: Maya

Maya is a 25-year-old woman with autism spectrum disorder and depression. She struggles with regulating her emotions and often feels overwhelmed by her feelings. Maya finds it difficult to participate in group therapy sessions because she feels anxious around others. The therapist adapts the interpersonal effectiveness module by providing Maya with individual therapy sessions and incorporating social stories and role-playing exercises into the therapy environment. The therapist also works with Maya to develop strategies for managing her depression, such as using a mood tracker and setting achievable goals for herself.

Case Study 11: Liam

Liam is a 21-year-old man with ADHD and substance use disorder. He struggles with regulating his emotions and often experiences intense mood swings. Liam finds it difficult to concentrate during therapy sessions and frequently interrupts others. The therapist adapts the emotion regulation module by providing Liam with visual aids, such as flowcharts and diagrams, to help him understand and remember the skills he has learned. The therapist also works with Liam to develop strategies for managing his impulsivity and avoiding triggers for substance use.

In summary, the neurodivergent-friendly approach to DBT involves adapting the therapy to meet the unique needs of individuals with neurodivergent conditions. This approach involves individualized treatment plans, sensory accommodations, flexibility and creativity, and emphasizing strengths. By adapting DBT in this way, individuals with neurodivergent conditions can more effectively learn skills to manage their emotions, regulate their behaviour, and improve their interpersonal relationships.

Chapter 2: What is neurodiversity

Neurodiversity is a concept that recognizes the natural variation in human neurology and the idea that neurological differences should be celebrated and valued, rather than stigmatized or pathologized. It recognizes that there is no "normal" or "typical" brain, and that each individual has unique strengths and challenges related to their neurological makeup.

The concept of neurodiversity emerged in the late 1990s as a response to the medical model of disability, which pathologizes neurological differences and views them as disorders or diseases that need to be cured or treated. Neurodiversity advocates argue that this model is stigmatizing and does not account for the benefits that neurodivergent individuals bring to society, such as creativity, innovation, and unique perspectives.

Neurodiversity encompasses a range of neurological differences, including autism spectrum disorder, attention deficit hyperactivity disorder (ADHD), dyslexia, Tourette syndrome, and others. These conditions are not considered as disorders or diseases by neurodiversity advocates, but rather as natural variations in human neurology that are shaped by both genetics and environment.

One of the key ideas behind neurodiversity is the social model of disability, which recognizes that disabilities are not solely caused by an individual's impairment, but also by the barriers in society that prevent individuals with impairments from fully participating and thriving. This model emphasizes the importance of creating a more inclusive and accessible society that values and accommodates individuals with different neurological profiles.

Neurodiversity advocates argue that society should move away from the medical model of disability and instead adopt a more inclusive and accepting perspective on neurological differences. This includes recognizing and valuing the unique strengths and abilities of neurodivergent individuals, and creating an environment that accommodates and supports these differences rather than trying to normalize or cure them.

While neurodiversity has gained significant attention in recent years, there are also some critiques of the concept. Some argue that it can downplay the challenges and difficulties that individuals with neurological differences may face, particularly when it comes to access to resources and support. Others argue that the concept may not be applicable to all neurological differences, particularly those that cause significant impairment or distress.

Despite these critiques, the concept of neurodiversity has helped to shift the discourse around neurological differences and disability, and has played a significant role in advocating for more inclusive and accessible societies.

By recognizing and celebrating the diversity of human neurology, neurodiversity offers a powerful tool for promoting social justice and creating a more accepting and accommodating world for all individuals, regardless of their neurological makeup.

Overview of common neurodivergent conditions

There are a number of common neurodivergent conditions that impact individuals in unique ways. These conditions can include autism spectrum disorder, attention deficit hyperactivity disorder (ADHD), dyslexia, and Tourette syndrome. While each of these conditions presents differently, they all share the characteristic of being neurological variations that impact how individuals perceive and interact with the world around them.

Autism Spectrum Disorder (ASD) Autism Spectrum Disorder is a condition that affects social interaction, communication, and behavior. Individuals with ASD may have difficulty with social communication and interaction, may have repetitive behaviors or narrow interests, and may be hypersensitive to sensory stimuli. For example, an individual with ASD may avoid eye contact or struggle with understanding social cues, making it difficult to connect with others.

Attention Deficit Hyperactivity Disorder (ADHD) ADHD is a condition that impacts an individual's ability to focus and control impulses. Individuals with ADHD may have difficulty with executive functioning skills such as planning and organization, time management, and prioritizing tasks. They may also struggle with emotional regulation and may be hyperactive or impulsive. For example, an individual with ADHD may have difficulty completing tasks or sitting still for long periods of time.

Dyslexia is a condition that impacts reading and language processing. Individuals with dyslexia may have difficulty recognizing and decoding words, and may struggle with spelling, reading fluency, and comprehension. They may also have difficulty with written expression. For example, an individual with dyslexia may have difficulty with reading assignments or writing essays.

Tourette Syndrome Tourette Syndrome is a condition that causes involuntary movements and vocalizations, known as tics. These tics may be simple or complex, and may be exacerbated by stress or anxiety. Individuals with Tourette syndrome may also have associated conditions such as ADHD or OCD. For example, an individual with Tourette syndrome may have difficulty controlling vocalizations or movements, which can impact social interactions and self-esteem.

It is important to note that while these conditions are often viewed as challenges, they can also bring unique strengths and abilities. For example, individuals with ASD may have exceptional memory skills or a unique perspective on complex problems, while individuals with ADHD may have high levels of energy and creativity. By recognizing and valuing these strengths, and providing appropriate support and accommodations for challenges, individuals with neurodivergent conditions can thrive in a variety of settings.

Neurodivergent and emotions

Neurodivergent individuals may experience emotions differently than neurotypical individuals due to differences in neurology, sensory processing, and social cognition. These differences can impact their ability to recognize and regulate their emotions, which can lead to challenges in social interactions, behavior, and mental health. Here are 10 case studies that illustrate how neurodivergent individuals may experience emotions differently and how this can impact their ability to regulate their emotions:

Case Study 1: Samantha Samantha is a 12-year-old girl with ADHD and sensory processing difficulties. She experiences emotions intensely and often feels overwhelmed by them. Samantha has difficulty recognizing when she is getting emotionally dysregulated and may have meltdowns or outbursts as a result. Her therapist works with her to identify her triggers and develop strategies for self-regulation, such as using a sensory tool or taking a break when she feels overwhelmed.

Case Study 2: Jackson Jackson is a 16-year-old boy with autism spectrum disorder. He struggles with recognizing and expressing his emotions, particularly when it comes to complex or nuanced feelings. Jackson may have difficulty understanding social cues related to emotions, which can impact his ability to form relationships and connect with others. His therapist works with him to develop a "feelings chart" that uses pictures to represent different emotions and to practice recognizing and expressing emotions in a safe and supportive environment.

Case Study 3: Maya Maya is a 23-year-old woman with dyslexia and depression. She struggles with regulating her emotions and often feels overwhelmed by her feelings. Maya has difficulty recognizing and articulating her emotions, which can make it challenging for her to receive appropriate support and treatment. Her therapist works with her to develop a personalized mood tracker and to practice identifying and labeling her emotions in therapy sessions.

Case Study 4: Ryan Ryan is a 14-year-old boy with Tourette syndrome and anxiety. He experiences intense emotions related to his tics and anxiety, and may feel embarrassed or ashamed as a result. Ryan may have difficulty regulating his emotions in social situations, which can impact his ability to form and maintain friendships. His therapist works with him to develop strategies for coping with anxiety and self-acceptance, such as using grounding techniques or practicing self-compassion.

Case Study 5: Eli Eli is a 19-year-old non-binary individual with ADHD and depression. They experience emotions intensely and may struggle with regulating their emotions in high-stress situations. Eli may also have difficulty recognizing when they need to take a break or seek support, which can impact their mental health. Their therapist works with them to develop personalized coping strategies, such as using a fidget toy or practicing mindfulness exercises, and to practice recognizing and expressing their emotions in a safe and supportive environment.

Case Study 6: Olivia Olivia is a 29-year-old woman with autism spectrum disorder and anxiety. She experiences emotions deeply and may struggle with regulating her emotions in social situations. Olivia may also have difficulty understanding social cues related to emotions, which can impact her ability to form and maintain relationships. Her therapist works with her to develop strategies for self-regulation, such as using a calming scent or taking a break when she feels overwhelmed, and to practice recognizing and labeling her emotions in therapy sessions.

Case Study 7: Andrew Andrew is a 22-year-old man with ADHD and substance use disorder. He experiences emotions intensely and may struggle with regulating his emotions in high-stress situations. Andrew may also use substances as a way to cope with his emotions, which can exacerbate his mental health challenges. His therapist works with him to develop strategies for self-regulation, such as practicing mindfulness exercises or using a mood tracker, and to address his substance use as a way to cope with emotional dysregulation.

Case Study 8: Rachel Rachel is a 27-year-old woman with dyslexia and borderline personality disorder (BPD). She experiences emotions intensely and may have difficulty regulating her emotions in relationships. Rachel may also struggle with identifying her emotions and may have a tendency to dissociate when overwhelmed. Her therapist works with her to develop personalized coping strategies, such as using a sensory tool or practicing self-validation, and to practice recognizing and labeling her emotions in therapy sessions.

Case Study 9: Ethan Ethan is a 10-year-old boy with ADHD and anxiety. He experiences emotions intensely and may struggle with regulating his emotions in high-stress situations, such as during a test or social event. Ethan may also have difficulty recognizing when he is getting emotionally dysregulated and may have outbursts or meltdowns as a result. His therapist works with him to develop strategies for self-regulation, such as using a fidget toy or taking a break when he feels overwhelmed, and to practice recognizing and expressing his emotions in a safe and supportive environment.

Case Study 10: Ava Ava is a 14-year-old girl with autism spectrum disorder and depression. She experiences emotions deeply but may have difficulty recognizing and articulating her emotions. Ava may also struggle with understanding social cues related to emotions, which can impact her ability to form and maintain relationships. Her therapist works with her to develop strategies for self-regulation, such as using a mood tracker or practicing mindfulness exercises, and to practice recognizing and expressing her emotions in therapy sessions.

In conclusion, neurodivergent individuals may experience emotions differently than neurotypical individuals due to differences in neurology, sensory processing, and social cognition. These differences can impact their ability to recognize and regulate their emotions, which can lead to challenges in social interactions, behavior, and mental health. However, with appropriate support and accommodations, neurodivergent individuals can learn to recognize and regulate their emotions in ways that work for them, and can thrive in a variety of settings.

Chapter 3: Mindfulness

Mindfulness is the practice of being present and fully engaged in the current moment, without judgment or distraction. It is an approach to mental health and well-being that has been shown to have many benefits for individuals with neurodivergent conditions, such as autism spectrum disorder, ADHD, and anxiety disorders. Here are some details about mindfulness and its benefits for neurodivergent individuals, as well as some examples of how it can be practiced:

Benefits of Mindfulness for Neurodivergent Individuals:

1. Improved emotional regulation: Mindfulness can help neurodivergent individuals to better recognize and regulate their emotions. It can provide a way for them to slow down and take stock of their feelings, rather than becoming overwhelmed by them. This can help to reduce the risk of emotional dysregulation, which can lead to negative outcomes such as meltdowns, outbursts, or self-harm.

2. Increased focus and attention: Mindfulness can help neurodivergent individuals to improve their ability to focus and attend to tasks. This can be particularly beneficial for individuals with ADHD, who may struggle with distractions and impulsivity. Mindfulness practice can help to strengthen the

neural pathways associated with attention and focus, making it easier to maintain attention over time.

3. Reduced anxiety and stress: Mindfulness has been shown to be an effective tool for reducing anxiety and stress in neurodivergent individuals. By cultivating a non-judgmental and accepting attitude towards their thoughts and feelings, individuals can learn to approach their anxiety and stress in a more positive and constructive way.

4. Improved social skills: Mindfulness can help neurodivergent individuals to improve their social skills, such as empathy and perspective-taking. By practicing mindfulness, individuals can learn to better understand their own emotions and the emotions of others, which can lead to more positive social interactions.

Examples of Mindfulness Practice for Neurodivergent Individuals:

1. Body scan: A body scan is a mindfulness exercise that involves focusing attention on different parts of the body, from the toes to the head. This can help neurodivergent individuals to become more aware of their physical sensations and to relax their body.

2. Breathing exercises: Breathing exercises can be a simple and effective way to practice mindfulness.

Neurodivergent individuals can try different techniques, such as counting breaths or focusing on the sensation of the breath moving in and out of the body.

3. Mindful walking: Mindful walking involves paying close attention to the physical sensations of walking, such as the movement of the feet and the sensation of the ground beneath them. This can help neurodivergent individuals to become more grounded and present in the moment.

4. Mindful eating: Mindful eating involves paying close attention to the sensory experience of eating, such as the taste, texture, and smell of the food. This can help neurodivergent individuals to become more aware of their hunger and fullness cues, and to enjoy their food in a more mindful way.

5. Mindful art: Mindful art involves engaging in creative activities, such as drawing or painting, in a mindful and non-judgmental way. This can help neurodivergent individuals to express their emotions and to engage in a calming and therapeutic activity.

Mindfulness exercises are a popular and effective tool for promoting mental health and well-being. These exercises involve paying attention to the present moment in a non-judgmental way, and can be adapted to meet the needs of individuals with different neurodivergent conditions. In this article, we will provide an overview of mindfulness exercises, and discuss how they can be adapted for individuals with conditions such as autism spectrum disorder, ADHD, and anxiety disorders. We will also provide 10 case studies to illustrate how mindfulness exercises can be applied in practice.

Overview of Mindfulness Exercises

There are many different mindfulness exercises that can be used to promote mental health and well-being. Here are some examples:

1. Breathing exercises: Breathing exercises involve paying attention to the sensation of the breath moving in and out of the body. This can help to promote relaxation and reduce stress.

2. Body scan: A body scan involves focusing attention on different parts of the body, from the toes to the head. This can help to promote awareness of physical sensations and relaxation.

3. Mindful eating: Mindful eating involves paying attention to the sensory experience of eating, such as the taste, texture, and smell of the food. This

can help to promote a healthy relationship with food and reduce overeating.

4. Mindful movement: Mindful movement involves paying attention to the physical sensations of movement, such as walking or yoga. This can help to promote relaxation and reduce stress.

5. Gratitude exercises: Gratitude exercises involve focusing on the things in life that we are grateful for, such as our relationships, health, or material possessions. This can help to promote a positive outlook and reduce negative emotions such as anxiety and depression.

Adapting Mindfulness Exercises for Different Neurodivergent Conditions:

1. Autism Spectrum Disorder (ASD): Individuals with ASD may struggle with social communication and interaction, and may have difficulty with sensory processing. To adapt mindfulness exercises for individuals with ASD, it is important to use clear and concrete language, and to provide sensory supports such as fidget toys or weighted blankets. Exercises such as mindful movement or body scan can be helpful for promoting relaxation and reducing anxiety.

2. Attention Deficit Hyperactivity Disorder (ADHD): Individuals with ADHD may struggle with attention and focus, and may have difficulty regulating their

emotions. To adapt mindfulness exercises for individuals with ADHD, it can be helpful to provide structured activities with clear goals and guidelines. Exercises such as breathing exercises or mindful movement can help to improve attention and focus.

3. Anxiety Disorders: Individuals with anxiety disorders may experience intense fear or worry that interferes with daily functioning. To adapt mindfulness exercises for individuals with anxiety disorders, it can be helpful to start with shorter and less intense exercises, and to provide reassurance and support throughout the process. Exercises such as breathing exercises or gratitude exercises can help to reduce anxiety and promote relaxation.

10 Case Studies:

1. Hannah is a 12-year-old girl with autism spectrum disorder. She struggles with sensory processing and often feels overwhelmed in social situations. Hannah's therapist works with her to develop a personalized body scan exercise that incorporates sensory supports such as a weighted blanket and calming music. Hannah practices this exercise before social events to help promote relaxation and reduce anxiety.

2. Max is a 9-year-old boy with ADHD. He struggles with attention and focus in school, and often feels

frustrated and overwhelmed. Max's therapist works with him to develop a breathing exercise that he can do during class breaks. Max practices this exercise every day to help improve his attention and reduce stress.

3. Emma is a 16-year-old girl with social anxiety disorder. She often feels nervous and self-conscious in social situations, and may avoid them altogether. Emma's therapist works with her to develop a gratitude exercise that focuses on the positive aspects of her life,Such as her close relationships with family and friends. Emma practices this exercise every day to help promote a positive outlook and reduce negative emotions such as anxiety.

4. Jack is a 14-year-old boy with Tourette syndrome. He experiences tics that can be socially embarrassing and may lead to feelings of shame or anxiety. Jack's therapist works with him to develop a breathing exercise that he can do whenever he feels the urge to tic. Jack practices this exercise regularly to help promote relaxation and reduce stress related to his tics.

5. Lily is a 20-year-old woman with ADHD and depression. She struggles with attention and focus, and may feel overwhelmed and helpless as a result. Lily's therapist works with her to develop a mindful movement exercise that she can do during study

breaks. Lily practices this exercise regularly to help improve her attention and focus, and to promote relaxation and reduce stress related to her depression.

6. Tom is a 25-year-old man with autism spectrum disorder and social anxiety disorder. He struggles with social communication and interaction, and may feel nervous and self-conscious in social situations. Tom's therapist works with him to develop a body scan exercise that incorporates visualization techniques to help him feel more comfortable and confident in social situations. Tom practices this exercise regularly to help promote relaxation and reduce anxiety.

7. Sarah is a 30-year-old woman with ADHD and anxiety. She struggles with attention and focus, and may feel overwhelmed and stressed as a result. Sarah's therapist works with her to develop a gratitude exercise that focuses on the positive aspects of her life, such as her job and her hobbies. Sarah practices this exercise regularly to help promote a positive outlook and reduce negative emotions such as anxiety.

8. Josh is a 16-year-old boy with autism spectrum disorder and depression. He struggles with social communication and interaction, and may feel isolated and lonely as a result. Josh's therapist works with him to develop a mindful movement

exercise that incorporates social interaction, such as partner yoga or dance. Josh practices this exercise regularly to help improve his social skills and promote relaxation and reduce stress related to his depression.

9. Rachel is a 14-year-old girl with dyslexia and anxiety. She struggles with attention and focus, and may feel overwhelmed and stressed in academic settings. Rachel's therapist works with her to develop a breathing exercise that she can do during class breaks. Rachel practices this exercise regularly to help improve her attention and focus, and to reduce stress related to her anxiety.

10. Mark is a 35-year-old man with ADHD and substance use disorder. He struggles with attention and focus, and may use substances as a way to cope with stress and negative emotions. Mark's therapist works with him to develop a mindfulness-based relapse prevention program, which incorporates mindfulness exercises such as breathing and body scan, as well as cognitive-behavioral therapy techniques to help him develop healthy coping strategies and reduce his substance use.

In conclusion, mindfulness is a valuable tool for neurodivergent individuals who may struggle with emotional regulation, attention, and social skills. By practicing mindfulness in a non-judgmental and accepting way, individuals can learn to approach their thoughts and feelings in a more positive and constructive way, which can lead to improved mental health and well-being. There are many different ways to practice mindfulness, and individuals can experiment with different techniques to find the ones that work best for them

How mindfulness can be used to regulate emotions and reduce stress

Mindfulness can be a valuable tool for regulating emotions and reducing stress in neurodivergent individuals. Neurodivergent individuals may experience emotions differently than neurotypical individuals and may struggle with emotional regulation. Here are some ways in which mindfulness can be used to regulate emotions and reduce stress in neurodivergent individuals:

1. Sensory Support: Neurodivergent individuals may benefit from incorporating sensory support into mindfulness practices. This can include using sensory objects such as weighted blankets or fidget toys, or incorporating sensory experiences such as aromatherapy or listening to calming music. These sensory supports can help to regulate emotions and promote relaxation.

2. Adapted Exercises: Mindfulness exercises can be adapted to meet the needs of neurodivergent individuals. For example, exercises such as body scanning or mindful observation can be adapted to

incorporate interests or sensory preferences of the individual. This can help to increase engagement and reduce stress.

3. Flexibility: Neurodivergent individuals may benefit from mindfulness practices that allow for flexibility and customization. This can include allowing for breaks or adjusting the length of mindfulness sessions to meet individual needs. This flexibility can help to reduce stress and promote engagement.

4. Emotion-Focused Techniques: Mindfulness techniques can be focused on specific emotions or experiences, such as anxiety or sensory overload. This can help neurodivergent individuals to become more aware of their emotions and develop strategies for regulating them.

Examples of mindfulness practices that can be adapted for neurodivergent individuals include:

1. Mindful Breathing: Mindful breathing is a simple and effective mindfulness technique that can be used to reduce stress and regulate emotions. By focusing on the breath, individuals can become more aware of their emotions and sensations in the present moment. One technique is to take a few slow, deep breaths, focusing on the sensation of the air moving in and out of the body.

2. Body Scan: Body scanning involves lying down and focusing on different parts of the body, starting at the toes and moving up towards the head. This technique can help individuals to become more aware of any physical sensations and tension in the body, which can be related to emotions and stress. By consciously relaxing each part of the body, individuals can reduce physical tension and promote relaxation.

3. Mindful Eating: Mindful eating involves paying attention to the sensations and experience of eating, including the taste, texture, and smell of the food. By focusing on the present moment and engaging the senses, individuals can reduce stress and regulate emotions. This technique can also promote healthier eating habits by encouraging individuals to eat more mindfully and intentionally.

4. Mindful Movement: Mindful movement involves engaging in physical activity while focusing on the present moment and bodily sensations. Examples include yoga, tai chi, or simply taking a walk while focusing on each step and the sensation of the body moving. This technique can reduce stress and promote relaxation by encouraging individuals to focus on the present moment and engage in physical activity.

5. Mindful Visualization: Mindful visualization involves imagining a peaceful scene or positive

outcome in the mind while focusing on the sensory details. This technique can be used to regulate emotions and reduce stress by promoting positive thinking and visualization.

6.   Mindful Journaling: Mindful journaling involves writing down thoughts and feelings without judgment or criticism. This technique can be used to regulate emotions by allowing individuals to become more aware of their thoughts and feelings and process them in a non-reactive way.

Overall, mindfulness practices can be adapted to meet the needs of neurodivergent individuals, providing valuable tools for emotional regulation and stress reduction. By incorporating sensory support, flexibility, and emotion-focused techniques, mindfulness can help neurodivergent individuals to develop greater self-awareness and emotional regulation skills, leading to greater well-being and quality of life.

Practice exercises for mindfulness

Sure, here are 30 mindfulness exercises that can be adapted for neurodivergent individuals, along with detailed explanations for each exercise:

1.   Mindful Breathing: Sit comfortably and focus your attention on your breath. Notice the sensation of the air moving in and out of your body. Count each inhale and exhale, focusing on the rhythm of your breath.

2. Body Scan: Lie down and close your eyes. Starting at your toes, slowly move your attention up your body, noticing any sensations or areas of tension. Relax each part of your body as you move up.

3. Mindful Observation: Choose an object and observe it for several minutes, noticing its colors, textures, and shapes. Pay close attention to any details that you may not have noticed before.

4. Mindful Walking: Take a walk outside and focus on each step you take. Notice the sensation of your feet touching the ground and the movement of your body as you walk.

5. Mindful Eating: Take a bite of food and savor it, paying attention to the flavor, texture, and sensation in your mouth. Chew slowly and notice how the food changes as you eat it.

6. Mindful Journaling: Take a few minutes to write down your thoughts and feelings, without judgment or criticism. Focus on the present moment and what is happening in your life right now.

7. Mindful Visualization: Close your eyes and visualize a peaceful scene, such as a beach or forest. Focus on the sensory details, such as the sound of the waves or the smell of the trees.

8. Mindful Listening: Choose a piece of music and listen to it without distraction. Pay attention to the different instruments and sounds, and how they blend together.

9. Mindful Coloring: Choose a coloring book or page and focus on the colors and shapes as you color. Pay attention to how your hand moves and the sensation of the pencil or marker.

10. Mindful Stretching: Stand up and stretch your body, paying attention to the sensations of your muscles as they lengthen and relax.

11. Mindful Breathing with Sensory Support: Use a breathing exercise with sensory support, such as holding a scented candle or using a weighted blanket. Focus on the sensation of the support as you breathe.

12. Mindful Body Scan with Sensory Support: Use a body scan exercise with sensory support, such as listening to calming music or using a fidget toy. Notice how the support affects your relaxation and attention.

13. Mindful Eating with Sensory Support: Use mindful eating with sensory support, such as using a particular utensil or dish that feels pleasant to hold. Focus on the sensory experience of the food as you eat it.

14. Mindful Movement with Sensory Support: Use a movement exercise with sensory support, such as using a balance board or exercising on a trampoline. Pay attention to the sensation of your body moving and how the support affects your balance.

15. Mindful Visualization with Sensory Support: Use a visualization exercise with sensory support, such as holding a crystal or other object that has personal significance. Focus on the sensory experience of the object as you visualize your peaceful scene.

16. Mindful Listening with Sensory Support: Use a listening exercise with sensory support, such as using noise-cancelling headphones or listening to music with deep bass. Focus on the sensation of the sound and how it affects your body.

17. Mindful Coloring with Sensory Support: Use a coloring exercise with sensory support, such as coloring on textured paper or using a particular type of pen or marker. Focus on the sensory experience of the colors and how they feel as you color.

18. Mindful Breathing with Movement: Combine breathing and movement by doing a simple yoga pose or stretch as you breathe.

19. Mindful Body Scan with Movement: Combine a body scan with movement by doing a simple yoga sequence or stretching as you move up your body. Focus on the sensations of your muscles as you stretch and relax.

20. Mindful Observation with Movement: Combine observation and movement by taking a nature walk and noticing the different plants and animals around you. Focus on the movement of your body and the sensory experience of the environment.

21. Mindful Eating with Movement: Combine mindful eating and movement by doing a simple yoga pose or stretch as you savor your food. Pay attention to the sensations in your body as you eat and move.

22. Mindful Visualization with Movement: Combine visualization and movement by imagining yourself in a peaceful scene while doing a simple yoga pose or stretch. Focus on the sensory experience of the environment and how it feels in your body.

23. Mindful Listening with Movement: Combine listening and movement by doing a simple dance or movement sequence as you listen to music. Pay attention to the sensations in your body as you move to the rhythm.

24. Mindful Coloring with Movement: Combine coloring and movement by doing a simple doodling or drawing exercise as you stretch or move your

body. Focus on the sensation of the pen or marker in your hand as you draw.

25. Mindful Breathing with Aromatherapy: Use a breathing exercise with aromatherapy, such as using an essential oil diffuser or inhaling a soothing scent. Focus on the sensation of the scent as you breathe.

26. Mindful Body Scan with Aromatherapy: Use a body scan exercise with aromatherapy, such as using a calming scent or essential oil as you relax your body. Notice how the scent affects your relaxation and attention.

27. Mindful Observation with Aromatherapy: Use observation exercise with aromatherapy, such as focusing on the colors and textures of flowers while inhaling their scent. Focus on the sensory experience of the scent and how it affects your mood.

28. Mindful Eating with Aromatherapy: Use mindful eating with aromatherapy, such as eating a meal or snack while enjoying the scent of a particular herb or spice. Focus on the sensory experience of the scent and taste of the food.

29. Mindful Visualization with Aromatherapy: Use a visualization exercise with aromatherapy, such as imagining yourself in a peaceful environment while inhaling a calming scent. Focus on the sensory

experience of the scent and how it affects your relaxation.

30. Mindful Listening with Aromatherapy: Use a listening exercise with aromatherapy, such as listening to calming music while diffusing a soothing scent. Pay attention to the sensory experience of the scent and how it affects your mood and relaxation.

Mindfulness exercises can be adapted in a variety of ways to meet the needs of neurodivergent individuals. By incorporating sensory support, movement, and other modifications, mindfulness can be a valuable tool for improving attention and focus, reducing stress and negative emotions, and promoting relaxation and overall well-being.

Chapter 4: Distress Tolerance

Distress tolerance is a concept in Dialectical Behaviour Therapy (DBT) that refers to an individual's ability to tolerate and manage distressing emotions, situations, and experiences. For neurodivergent individuals who may struggle with emotional regulation or sensory overload, distress tolerance skills can be particularly helpful in managing intense emotions and reducing stress. In this article, we will explore the benefits of distress tolerance for neurodivergent individuals and provide six case studies to illustrate its application in practice.

Benefits of Distress Tolerance for Neurodivergent Individuals

1. Improved Emotional Regulation: Distress tolerance skills can help neurodivergent individuals to regulate their emotions by allowing them to tolerate and manage difficult emotions without becoming overwhelmed. This can lead to greater emotional stability and an increased ability to cope with stress.

2. Reduced Impulsivity: Neurodivergent individuals may be more prone to impulsivity or acting on impulse in response to distressing situations. Distress tolerance skills can help individuals to pause and think before acting, reducing impulsivity

and promoting more thoughtful and effective decision-making.

3. Increased Resilience: Distress tolerance skills can help neurodivergent individuals to develop greater resilience by learning how to tolerate and manage difficult emotions and experiences. This can lead to increased self-confidence and a greater ability to cope with adversity.

4. Improved Interpersonal Relationships: By developing greater distress tolerance skills, neurodivergent individuals can improve their ability to communicate effectively and manage conflict in interpersonal relationships. This can lead to more positive and fulfilling relationships.

5. Reduced Stress: Distress tolerance skills can help neurodivergent individuals to reduce stress by promoting mindfulness and relaxation techniques. This can lead to increased well-being and a greater ability to cope with challenging situations.

Case Studies

1. Sarah is a 30-year-old woman with ADHD who struggles with impulsive behaviour and difficulty regulating her emotions. Through DBT, she learned distress tolerance skills such as distraction techniques, self-soothing, and mindfulness. When she experiences distressing emotions or situations, she now has the tools to regulate her emotions and

make thoughtful decisions rather than acting impulsively.

2. David is a 16-year-old boy with autism spectrum disorder who experiences sensory overload in social situations. Through DBT, he learned distress tolerance skills such as breathing techniques, grounding exercises, and sensory supports. He now has the tools to manage his sensory overload and reduce stress in social situations.

3. Marie is a 25-year-old woman with dyslexia who experiences anxiety and difficulty with decision-making. Through DBT, she learned distress tolerance skills such as problem-solving techniques, emotion-focused coping, and visualization. She now has the tools to manage her anxiety and make thoughtful decisions without becoming overwhelmed.

4. James is a 40-year-old man with Tourette syndrome who experiences tics and social anxiety. Through DBT, he learned distress tolerance skills such as acceptance techniques, mindfulness, and social skills training. He now has the tools to manage his tics and anxiety in social situations and improve his overall quality of life.

5. Maya is a 12-year-old girl with ADHD who struggles with emotional dysregulation and impulsivity. Through DBT, she learned distress tolerance skills

such as cognitive restructuring, problem-solving techniques, and mindfulness. She now has the tools to regulate her emotions and make thoughtful decisions in response to distressing situations.

6. John is a 35-year-old man with dyslexia who experiences stress and overwhelm in work situations. Through DBT, he learned distress tolerance skills such as time management techniques, emotion-focused coping, and mindfulness. He now has the tools to manage his stress and reduce overwhelm in the workplace.

In conclusion, distress tolerance skills can be a valuable tool for neurodivergent individuals who may struggle with emotional regulation, sensory overload, and impulsivity. Through distress tolerance skills, individuals can learn how to tolerate and manage difficult emotions and experiences, reduce impulsivity, increase resilience, improve interpersonal relationships, and reduce stress. Distress tolerance skills can be tailored to meet the specific needs of neurodivergent individuals, such as incorporating sensory supports or adapting techniques to accommodate sensory sensitivities. The case studies above illustrate the diverse range of neurodivergent individuals who can benefit from distress tolerance skills and the specific techniques and strategies used to support their needs.

Overall, incorporating distress tolerance skills into therapeutic interventions, such as DBT, can be a powerful tool for supporting the emotional well-being and overall quality of life of neurodivergent individuals. By developing greater distress tolerance skills, individuals can learn how to manage difficult emotions and experiences in a more effective and resilient manner, leading to greater overall well-being and life satisfaction.

Adapting distress tolerance skills for different neurodivergent conditions

Distress tolerance skills are strategies and techniques that can help individuals cope with distressing emotions and situations. These skills are a key component of Dialectical Behavior Therapy (DBT), a type of cognitive-behavioral therapy that was originally developed to treat individuals with borderline personality disorder. Distress tolerance skills can be adapted to meet the specific needs of individuals with different neurodivergent conditions. Here is an overview of distress tolerance skills and how they can be adapted for different neurodivergent conditions, along with six case studies to illustrate their application.

Distress Tolerance Skills and Adaptations for Neurodivergent Conditions

1. Mindfulness: Mindfulness is a core distress tolerance skill that involves focusing on the present moment without judgment or distraction. Mindfulness techniques can be adapted for neurodivergent individuals by incorporating sensory supports such as weighted blankets or

fidget toys, or by incorporating sensory experiences such as aromatherapy or listening to calming music. This can be particularly helpful for individuals with autism spectrum disorder who may struggle with sensory overload.

2. Self-Soothing: Self-soothing is a distress tolerance skill that involves engaging in activities that promote relaxation and comfort. Self-soothing techniques can be adapted for neurodivergent individuals by incorporating sensory supports such as weighted blankets or calming scents, or by engaging in activities that are soothing and calming such as taking a bath or going for a walk. This can be particularly helpful for individuals with Tourette syndrome who may experience tics or sensory overload.

3. Grounding: Grounding is a distress tolerance skill that involves focusing on the present moment by connecting to the senses. Grounding techniques can be adapted for neurodivergent individuals by incorporating sensory supports such as fidget toys or aromatherapy, or by focusing on specific sensory experiences such as the feeling of the ground beneath one's feet or the taste of a favorite food. This can be particularly helpful for individuals with dyslexia who may experience anxiety or difficulty with decision-making.

4. Problem-Solving: Problem-solving is a distress tolerance skill that involves identifying and implementing solutions to difficult situations or problems. Problem-solving techniques can be adapted for neurodivergent individuals by incorporating tools such as visual aids or structured decision-making processes, or by breaking down problems into smaller, more manageable parts. This can be particularly helpful for individuals with ADHD who may struggle with impulsivity or decision-making.

5. Acceptance: Acceptance is a distress tolerance skill that involves accepting difficult emotions or situations without judgment. Acceptance techniques can be adapted for neurodivergent individuals by incorporating mindfulness or sensory supports, or by focusing on specific emotions or experiences. This can be particularly helpful for individuals with anxiety or depression who may struggle with acceptance or self-compassion.

6. Distraction: Distraction is a distress tolerance skill that involves shifting attention away from distressing thoughts or emotions. Distraction techniques can be adapted for neurodivergent individuals by incorporating sensory supports or interests, or by engaging in activities that promote focus or creativity. This can be particularly helpful for individuals with ADHD or sensory sensitivities.

Case Studies

1. Emily is a 25-year-old woman with autism spectrum disorder who struggles with sensory overload. She learned mindfulness techniques that incorporated sensory supports such as a weighted blanket and calming scents. By incorporating these supports, she was able to focus on the present moment and manage her sensory overload.

2. Ben is a 30-year-old man with Tourette syndrome who experiences tics in social situations. He learned self-soothing techniques such as taking deep breaths or engaging in calming activities like listening to music. By using these techniques, he was able to manage his tics and reduce his anxiety in social situations.

3. Tom is a 16-year-old boy with dyslexia who experiences anxiety and difficulty with decision-making. He learned grounding techniques that incorporated sensory supports such as a fidget toy and focused on specific sensory experiences such as the feeling of the ground beneath his feet. By using these techniques, he was able to manage his anxiety and make more thoughtful decisions.

4. Alice is a 40-year-old woman with ADHD who struggles with impulsivity. She learned problem-solving techniques that incorporated visual aids and structured decision-making processes. By using these techniques, she was able to break down

problems into more manageable parts and make more thoughtful decisions.

5. Sam is a 35-year-old man with anxiety who struggles with self-acceptance. He learned acceptance techniques that incorporated mindfulness and focused on specific emotions or experiences. By using these techniques, he was able to accept difficult emotions and practice self-compassion.

6. Maria is a 12-year-old girl with sensory sensitivities who experiences overwhelm in crowded environments. She learned distraction techniques that incorporated sensory interests such as coloring or engaging in calming activities like breathing exercises. By using these techniques, she was able to shift her attention away from overwhelming stimuli and manage her sensory sensitivities.

Distress tolerance skills can be a valuable tool for neurodivergent individuals in managing distressing emotions and situations. By adapting distress tolerance techniques to meet the specific needs of individuals with different neurodivergent conditions, therapists can help their clients to develop effective coping strategies and improve their emotional regulation. The case studies above illustrate the diverse range of neurodivergent individuals who can benefit from distress tolerance skills and the specific techniques and strategies used to support their needs.

Distress tolerance and overwhelming emotions

Distress tolerance skills are important for managing overwhelming emotions and crises, and can be particularly helpful for individuals with neurodivergent conditions. Dialectical Behavior Therapy (DBT) is a type of therapy that incorporates distress tolerance skills to help individuals manage difficult emotions and situations. Here are six case studies that illustrate how distress tolerance skills can be used to manage overwhelming emotions and crises.

1. Jane is a 27-year-old woman with borderline personality disorder who experiences intense emotions and struggles with impulsivity. During a recent crisis, she utilized distress tolerance skills she learned in DBT, including deep breathing and progressive muscle relaxation. She was able to stay present and grounded during the crisis, which helped her to manage her emotions and make a thoughtful decision.

2. John is a 35-year-old man with ADHD who experiences intense anger and frustration when things don't go according to plan. During a recent crisis at work, he utilized distress tolerance skills such as taking a break to go for a walk and engaging in calming activities like listening to music. These techniques helped him to manage his

anger and frustration and approach the situation with a more clear and thoughtful mindset.

3. Sarah is a 22-year-old woman with autism spectrum disorder who experiences sensory overload in overwhelming situations. During a recent crisis at a crowded event, she utilized distress tolerance skills such as focusing on her breath and using sensory supports like noise-canceling headphones. These techniques helped her to manage her sensory overload and remain present and grounded during the crisis.

4. David is a 30-year-old man with Tourette syndrome who experiences intense tics during stressful situations. During a recent crisis at work, he utilized distress tolerance skills such as progressive muscle relaxation and engaging in calming activities like deep breathing. These techniques helped him to manage his tics and approach the situation with a more clear and thoughtful mindset.

5. Karen is a 40-year-old woman with dyslexia who experiences anxiety and overwhelm when facing new challenges. During a recent crisis involving a new job opportunity, she utilized distress tolerance skills such as problem-solving and breaking down the challenge into smaller, more manageable parts. These techniques helped her to manage her anxiety and approach the situation with a more clear and thoughtful mindset.

6. Alex is a 15-year-old boy with sensory sensitivities who experiences overwhelm and shutdown during stressful situations. During a recent crisis at school, he utilized distress tolerance skills such as distraction techniques like focusing on a calming sensory experience or engaging in a favorite hobby. These techniques helped him to manage his overwhelm and approach the situation with a more clear and thoughtful mindset.

In conclusion, distress tolerance skills can be a valuable tool for managing overwhelming emotions and crises for individuals with neurodivergent conditions. The case studies above illustrate how distress tolerance techniques can be adapted to meet the specific needs of individuals with different neurodivergent conditions and help them to manage their emotions and approach difficult situations with more clarity and thoughtfulness.

Practice exercises for distress tolerance

Self-soothing with senses: Engage in activities that stimulate your senses, such as smelling lavender or taking a warm bath.

Result: Self-soothing with senses can help to reduce emotional distress by providing comfort and relaxation.

2. **Mindful breathing**: Focus on your breath as it enters and leaves your body, taking deep breaths in and out.

Result: Mindful breathing can help to reduce stress and anxiety by bringing your attention to the present moment and calming the mind.

3. **Positive self-talk**: Use positive and encouraging language when speaking to yourself.

Result: Positive self-talk can help to increase self-esteem and reduce negative self-talk.

4. **Distraction techniques**: Engage in activities that distract you from distressing thoughts or emotions, such as reading a book or watching a movie.

Result: Distraction techniques can help to reduce emotional distress by redirecting your attention to something else.

5. **Radical acceptance**: Acknowledge and accept the reality of a situation that cannot be changed.

Result: Radical acceptance can help to reduce emotional distress by promoting a sense of peace and allowing for greater emotional regulation.

6. **Create a crisis plan**: Develop a plan for how to manage crises or difficult situations.

Result: A crisis plan can help to reduce stress and anxiety by providing a sense of preparedness and control.

7. **Physical activity**: Engage in physical activity, such as going for a walk or doing yoga.

Result: Physical activity can help to reduce stress and increase feelings of well-being.

8. **Progressive muscle relaxation**: Tense and relax different muscle groups in your body, starting from your feet and working your way up.

Result: Progressive muscle relaxation can help to reduce physical tension and promote relaxation.

9. **Meditation**: Sit quietly and focus on your breath or a mantra.

Result: Meditation can help to promote relaxation and reduce stress and anxiety.

10. **Engage in a hobby**: Participate in a hobby that you enjoy, such as painting or playing music.

Result: Engaging in a hobby can help to distract from distressing thoughts and promote feelings of enjoyment and fulfillment.

11. **Social support**: Reach out to friends, family, or a therapist for support.

Result: Social support can help to reduce feelings of isolation and provide emotional validation and comfort.

12. **Identify coping thoughts**: Identify thoughts that can help you cope with distressing situations, such as "I can get through this."

Result: Identifying coping thoughts can help to increase emotional regulation and reduce distress.

13. **Emotion regulation skills**: Learn skills to regulate emotions, such as deep breathing or grounding techniques.

Result: Emotion regulation skills can help to reduce emotional distress and increase emotional regulation.

14. **Practice self-care**: Engage in activities that promote self-care, such as taking a warm bath or practicing yoga.

Result: Practicing self-care can help to reduce stress and promote feelings of well-being.

15. **Take a break**: Step away from a distressing situation and take a break to relax and recharge.

Result: Taking a break can help to reduce stress and promote emotional regulation.

16. **Use humor**: Find humor in a difficult situation to promote emotional regulation and reduce distress.

Result: Using humor can help to reduce emotional distress and promote a more positive outlook.

17. **Use mindfulness**: Practice mindfulness to increase awareness of the present moment and reduce emotional distress.

Result: Mindfulness can help to promote relaxation and reduce stress and anxiety.

18. **Engage in creative expression**: Engage in creative activities, such as drawing or writing, to promote emotional expression and reduce distress.

Result: Engaging in creative expression can help to reduce emotional distress

19. **Use a stress ball**: Squeeze a stress ball to release physical tension and promote relaxation.

Result: Using a stress ball can help to reduce physical tension and promote relaxation.

20. **Engage in physical touch**: Give yourself a hug or wrap yourself in a blanket to provide comfort and a sense of security.

Result: Engaging in physical touch can help to reduce emotional distress by providing a sense of comfort and security.

21. **Create a gratitude list**: Write down things you are grateful for to promote positive emotions and reduce distress.

Result: Creating a gratitude list can help to increase positive emotions and promote a sense of well-being.

22. **Engage in deep breathing**: Take deep breaths in and out to promote relaxation and reduce stress.

Result: Deep breathing can help to reduce stress and promote relaxation.

23. **Use visualization**: Visualize a calming scene or situation to promote relaxation and reduce emotional distress.

Result: Visualization can help to promote relaxation and reduce emotional distress.

24. **Use a mantra**: Repeat a positive or calming phrase to promote emotional regulation and reduce distress.

Result: Using a mantra can help to promote emotional regulation and reduce emotional distress.

25. **Engage in grounding techniques**: Use grounding techniques, such as focusing on the present moment or sensory stimulation, to promote emotional regulation and reduce distress.

Result: Grounding techniques can help to increase emotional regulation and reduce emotional distress.

26. **Practice radical forgiveness**: Practice forgiveness of oneself or others to reduce emotional distress and promote emotional healing.

Result: Practicing radical forgiveness can help to reduce emotional distress and promote emotional healing.

27. **Engage in positive self-affirmations**: Use positive self-talk to promote self-esteem and reduce negative self-talk.

Result: Engaging in positive self-affirmations can help to increase self-esteem and reduce negative self-talk.

28. **Engage in progressive exposure**: Gradually expose oneself to a distressing situation to promote emotional regulation and reduce distress.

Result: Engaging in progressive exposure can help to increase emotional regulation and reduce emotional distress.

29. **Use a stress ball**: Squeeze a stress ball to release physical tension and promote relaxation.

Result: Using a stress ball can help to reduce physical tension and promote relaxation.

30. **Engage in self-compassion**: Practice self-compassion by treating oneself with kindness and understanding.

Result: Engaging in self-compassion can help to reduce emotional distress and promote a sense of well-being.

Chapter 5: Emotion Regulation

Emotion regulation and its benefits for neurodivergent individuals

Emotion regulation is the ability to effectively manage and modulate one's emotions in response to different situations. It is an important skill that can help individuals cope with stress, regulate mood, and improve overall well-being. For neurodivergent individuals, who may experience emotions differently or struggle with emotional regulation, developing emotion regulation skills can be particularly beneficial.

Benefits of emotion regulation for neurodivergent individuals may include:

1. Improved mood and overall well-being

2. Reduced emotional distress and anxiety

3. Increased ability to manage stress

4. Improved interpersonal relationships

5. Increased self-awareness and self-control

Overview of emotion regulation skills and how to adapt them for different neurodivergent conditions:

Emotion regulation skills can be adapted for different neurodivergent conditions based on individual needs and preferences. Some examples of emotion regulation skills that may be helpful for neurodivergent individuals include:

1. Mindfulness: Practicing mindfulness can help individuals become more aware of their thoughts and feelings, which can promote emotional regulation and reduce emotional distress.

2. Cognitive reappraisal: Reframing negative thoughts or situations in a more positive light can help to reduce emotional distress and promote a more positive outlook.

3. Self-compassion: Practicing self-compassion and treating oneself with kindness and understanding can promote emotional regulation and reduce negative self-talk.

4. Positive self-talk: Using positive and encouraging language when speaking to oneself can help to increase self-esteem and reduce negative self-talk.

5. Problem-solving: Developing effective problem-solving skills can help individuals manage stress and reduce emotional distress.

6. Acceptance: Accepting and acknowledging difficult emotions can help to promote emotional regulation and reduce emotional distress.

Case studies:

1. Mark, a young adult with autism, struggles with intense emotions that can lead to outbursts and meltdowns. Through therapy, he learns to practice mindfulness and use deep breathing techniques to regulate his emotions and reduce stress.

2. Jessica, a teenager with ADHD, often feels overwhelmed and anxious in social situations. With the help of a therapist, she learns cognitive reappraisal techniques to reframe her negative thoughts and reduce social anxiety.

3. Jamal, a child with dyslexia, experiences frustration and anger when he struggles with reading and writing. With the help of a therapist, he learns self-compassion techniques to treat himself with kindness and understanding, which helps to reduce his emotional distress.

4. Maria, a young adult with Tourette syndrome, experiences anxiety and embarrassment related to her tics. With the help of a therapist, she learns problem-solving techniques to manage her stress and reduce emotional distress related to her tics.

5. Michael, a young adult with OCD, experiences intense anxiety related to intrusive thoughts and compulsions. Through therapy, he learns acceptance techniques to acknowledge and accept

his difficult emotions, which helps to reduce emotional distress.

6. Rachel, a teenager with Asperger's syndrome, struggles with emotional regulation and often feels overwhelmed and anxious in social situations. With the help of a therapist, she learns emotion regulation techniques, including mindfulness and positive self-talk, to help manage her emotions and reduce stress.

7. Jack, a child with ADHD, often feels restless and has difficulty focusing. Through therapy, he learns mindfulness techniques to help him stay present in the moment and reduce distraction.

8. Sarah, a teenager with autism, struggles with sensory overload and can become easily overwhelmed in loud or chaotic environments. With the help of a therapist, she learns emotion regulation techniques, including mindfulness and deep breathing, to help manage her emotions and reduce distress in sensory overload situations.

9. Kyle, a young adult with dyslexia, often feels frustrated and embarrassed when he struggles with reading and writing. With the help of a therapist, he learns cognitive reappraisal techniques to reframe his negative thoughts and increase his self-esteem.

10. Samantha, a child with Tourette syndrome, experiences anxiety and embarrassment related to her tics. With the help of a therapist, she learns mindfulness techniques to help her stay present in the moment and reduce emotional distress related to her tics.

11. Adam, a young adult with OCD, experiences intense anxiety related to his compulsions. Through therapy, he learns acceptance techniques to acknowledge and accept his difficult emotions, which helps to reduce emotional distress.

12. Haley, a teenager with ADHD, often feels overwhelmed and anxious in academic settings. With the help of a therapist, she learns emotion regulation techniques, including mindfulness and positive self-talk, to help manage her emotions and reduce stress in academic situations.

In summary, emotion regulation skills can be helpful for neurodivergent individuals to manage their emotions, reduce emotional distress, and improve overall well-being. These skills can be adapted to meet individual needs and preferences and can be learned through therapy or self-help techniques. The case studies provide examples of how emotion regulation skills can be applied in different contexts and for different neurodivergent conditions.

Emotion Regulation exercises

1. **Identify triggers**: Keep a log of situations or events that trigger intense emotions, then develop a plan to manage those triggers.

Result: Identifying triggers can help individuals to better manage their emotions and reduce emotional distress.

2. **Practice positive self-talk**: Use positive and encouraging language when speaking to oneself to increase self-esteem and reduce negative self-talk.

Result: Practicing positive self-talk can help to promote emotional regulation and reduce emotional distress.

3. **Create a coping toolbox**: Develop a list of coping strategies and tools, such as deep breathing or mindfulness exercises, to use during times of emotional distress.

Result: Creating a coping toolbox can help individuals to effectively manage their emotions and reduce emotional distress.

4. **Engage in progressive muscle relaxation**: Tighten and relax different muscle groups to promote relaxation and reduce physical tension associated with emotional distress.

Result: Engaging in progressive muscle relaxation can help to reduce physical tension and promote relaxation.

5. **Use positive imagery**: Visualize positive outcomes or situations to promote emotional regulation and reduce emotional distress.

Result: Using positive imagery can help to increase positive emotions and reduce emotional distress.

6. **Practice self-compassion**: Treat oneself with kindness and understanding to promote emotional regulation and reduce negative self-talk.

Result: Practicing self-compassion can help to increase emotional regulation and reduce emotional distress.

7. **Use mindfulness techniques**: Practice mindfulness exercises to become more aware of thoughts and feelings and promote emotional regulation.

Result: Using mindfulness techniques can help to increase emotional regulation and reduce emotional distress.

8. **Engage in physical activity**: Exercise can help to release endorphins and promote positive emotions, reducing emotional distress.

Result: Engaging in physical activity can help to increase positive emotions and reduce emotional distress.

9. **Create a gratitude list**: Write down things one is grateful for to promote positive emotions and reduce distress.

Result: Creating a gratitude list can help to increase positive emotions and promote a sense of well-being.

10. **Develop assertiveness skills**: Practice assertiveness techniques to effectively communicate needs and boundaries and reduce emotional distress related to conflict.

Result: Developing assertiveness skills can help to reduce emotional distress related to conflict and promote positive interpersonal relationships.

11. **Practice problem-solving skills**: Develop effective problem-solving skills to manage stress and reduce emotional distress.

Result: Practicing problem-solving skills can help individuals to effectively manage stress and reduce emotional distress.

12. **Engage in deep breathing**: Take deep breaths in and out to promote relaxation and reduce stress.

Result: Engaging in deep breathing can help to reduce stress and promote relaxation.

13. **Identify and challenge negative thoughts**: Recognize negative thought patterns and challenge them with evidence-based reasoning to promote emotional regulation and reduce emotional distress.

Result: Identifying and challenging negative thoughts can help to promote emotional regulation and reduce emotional distress.

14. **Practice radical acceptance**: Accept difficult emotions or situations without judgment to promote emotional regulation and reduce emotional distress.

Result: Practicing radical acceptance can help to reduce emotional distress and promote emotional healing.

15. **Engage in social support**: Connect with friends or family members for emotional support and to promote positive emotions.

Result: Engaging in social support can help to increase positive emotions and reduce emotional distress.

16. **Set achievable goals**: Develop realistic goals and action plans to promote a sense of accomplishment and reduce emotional distress related to feeling overwhelmed.

Result: Setting achievable goals can help to promote a sense of accomplishment and reduce emotional distress related to feeling overwhelmed.

17. **Practice gratitude journaling**: Write down things one is grateful for to promote positive emotions and reduce emotional distress.

Result: Practicing gratitude journaling can help to increase positive emotions and promote a sense of well-being.

18. **Engage in creative expression**: Use creative outlets, such as art music, or writing, to promote emotional regulation and reduce emotional distress.

19. Result: Engaging in creative expression can help to increase positive emotions and promote a sense of well-being.

20. **Engage in sensory activities**: Use sensory activities, such as sensory bins or weighted blankets, to promote relaxation and reduce emotional distress related to sensory overload.

21. Result: Engaging in sensory activities can help to reduce emotional distress related to sensory overload and promote relaxation.

22. **Use grounding techniques**: Practice grounding exercises, such as focusing on sensory input or repeating a calming phrase, to promote emotional regulation and reduce emotional distress.

23. Result: Using grounding techniques can help to promote emotional regulation and reduce emotional distress.

In summary, emotion regulation exercises can be adapted for different neurodivergent individuals based on individual needs and preferences. These exercises can help individuals to manage their emotions, reduce emotional distress, and improve overall well-being. The exercises provided offer a variety of techniques and strategies for promoting emotional regulation, from mindfulness and deep breathing to gratitude journaling and creative expression. By incorporating these exercises into their daily routine, neurodivergent individuals can develop the skills necessary to manage their emotions and thrive in their daily lives.

Chapter 6: Interpersonal Effectiveness

Interpersonal effectiveness refers to the ability to communicate and interact effectively with others, while also maintaining one's own values and boundaries. It involves the development of skills such as assertiveness, effective communication, and conflict resolution. For neurodivergent individuals, who may struggle with social cues and communication, developing interpersonal effectiveness skills can be particularly beneficial.

Benefits of interpersonal effectiveness for neurodivergent individuals include improved communication and social skills, increased confidence in social situations, and the ability to establish and maintain healthy relationships. These skills can also help individuals to navigate social situations with more ease, reducing social anxiety and promoting a sense of belonging.

Interpersonal effectiveness skills can be adapted for different neurodivergent conditions based on individual needs and preferences. For example, for individuals with autism spectrum disorder (ASD), social scripts and visual supports may be particularly helpful in developing communication and social skills. For individuals with ADHD, skills such as time management and organizational strategies can be helpful in maintaining healthy relationships and avoiding conflicts.

Interpersonal effectiveness skills may include:

1. **Assertiveness**: The ability to communicate one's needs and boundaries effectively while also respecting the needs and boundaries of others. Assertiveness skills can help individuals to establish and maintain healthy relationships while avoiding conflicts.

2. **Effective communication**: The ability to express oneself clearly and effectively while also listening actively to others. Effective communication skills can help individuals to build positive relationships and avoid misunderstandings.

3. **Active listening**: The ability to listen to others and understand their perspective while also expressing empathy and validating their feelings. Active listening skills can help individuals to establish rapport and build trust in their relationships.

4. **Conflict resolution**: The ability to identify and address conflicts effectively while also maintaining healthy relationships. Conflict resolution skills can help individuals to navigate difficult situations and avoid harmful outcomes.

5. **Boundary-setting**: The ability to establish and maintain personal boundaries while also respecting the boundaries of others. Boundary-setting skills can help individuals to maintain healthy relationships and avoid conflicts.

6. **Negotiation**: The ability to find mutually beneficial solutions to conflicts and disagreements. Negotiation skills can help individuals to build positive relationships and avoid conflicts.

Cases studies of Interpersonal effectiveness

1. John is a 25-year-old with ADHD who struggles with assertiveness in his work environment. Through therapy, he learns to use "I" statements and establish boundaries with his colleagues. As a result, he feels more confident in expressing his needs and maintaining positive relationships at work.

2. Sarah is a 30-year-old with autism spectrum disorder (ASD) who has difficulty with effective communication. She works with a therapist to improve her social skills, including maintaining eye contact and using appropriate body language. As a result, she feels more confident in her social interactions and is able to build stronger relationships.

3. Ben is a 16-year-old with dyslexia who struggles with active listening. He works with a tutor to practice listening skills, including repeating back what was said and asking clarifying questions. As a result, he is able to improve his grades and build stronger relationships with his teachers.

4. Samantha is a 20-year-old with Tourette syndrome who struggles with conflict resolution. She works with a therapist to practice mindfulness techniques and learn to manage her tics during difficult conversations. As a result, she is able to navigate conflicts more effectively and maintain healthier relationships.

5. Mike is a 40-year-old with OCD who struggles with boundary-setting in his personal relationships. He works with a therapist to establish clear boundaries with his friends and family and practice self-care techniques to manage his anxiety. As a result, he is able to maintain healthier relationships and feel more confident in his social interactions.

6. Lisa is a 28-year-old with ADHD who struggles with negotiation in her professional life. She works with a career coach to develop negotiation strategies and practice self-advocacy. As a result, she is able to secure a higher salary and build stronger relationships with her colleagues.

7. Tim is a 35-year-old with ASD who struggles with assertiveness in his personal relationships. He works with a therapist to develop social scripts and practice assertiveness techniques in low-pressure situations. As a result, he is able to communicate his needs and maintain healthier relationships with his friends and family.

8. Rachel is a 22-year-old with dyslexia who struggles with effective communication in her academic life. She works with a tutor to practice written communication skills and develop organization strategies for her schoolwork. As a result, she is able to improve her grades and build stronger relationships with her teachers.

9. Chris is a 30-year-old with Tourette syndrome who struggles with active listening in his personal relationships. He works with a therapist to develop techniques for managing his tics during conversations and practicing active listening skills. As a result, he is able to build stronger relationships with his friends and family.

10. Olivia is a 27-year-old with OCD who struggles with conflict resolution in her work environment. She works with a therapist to develop coping strategies for managing anxiety during difficult conversations and practicing assertiveness techniques. As a result, she is able to navigate conflicts more effectively and maintain positive relationships with her colleagues.

11. Jake is a 18-year-old with ADHD who struggles with boundary-setting in his personal relationships. He works with a therapist to develop strategies for setting boundaries with his friends and family and practicing self-care techniques to manage his anxiety. As a result, he is able to maintain healthier

relationships and feel more confident in his social interactions.

12. Michelle is a 35-year-old with ASD who struggles with negotiation in her professional life. She works with a career coach to develop negotiation strategies and practice self-advocacy. As a result, she is able to secure a promotion and build stronger relationships with her colleagues.

13. David is a 25-year-old with dyslexia who struggles with effective communication in his personal relationships. He works with a therapist to practice communication skills, including active listening and expressing empathy. As a result, he is able to build stronger relationships with his friends and family.

14. Emily is a 20-year-old with Tourette syndrome who struggles with conflict resolution in her personal relationships. She works with a therapist to practice mindfulness techniques and develop coping strategies for managing her tics during difficult conversations. As a result, she is able to navigate conflicts more effectively and maintain healthier relationships.

15. Alex is a 30-year-old with ADHD who struggles with assertiveness in his work environment. He works with a therapist to develop assertiveness techniques, including using "I" statements and standing up for himself in professional situations.

As a result, he is able to communicate his needs effectively and maintain positive relationships with his colleagues.

16. Rebecca is a 22-year-old with OCD who struggles with boundary-setting in her personal relationships. She works with a therapist to establish clear boundaries with her friends and family and practice self-care techniques to manage her anxiety. As a result, she is able to maintain healthier relationships and feel more confident in social situations.

17. Tyler is a 18-year-old with ASD who struggles with effective communication in his academic life. He works with a tutor to practice social skills, including maintaining eye contact and using appropriate body language. As a result, he is able to build stronger relationships with his teachers and peers.

18. Sarah is a 35-year-old with dyslexia who struggles with active listening in her personal relationships. She works with a therapist to develop techniques for managing distractions during conversations and practicing active listening skills. As a result, she is able to build stronger relationships with her friends and family.

19. Mark is a 28-year-old with ADHD who struggles with conflict resolution in his personal relationships. He works with a therapist to develop

coping strategies for managing his impulsivity during difficult conversations and practicing effective communication skills. As a result, he is able to navigate conflicts more effectively and maintain healthier relationships.

20. Lily is a 25-year-old with Tourette syndrome who struggles with negotiation in her professional life. She works with a career coach to develop negotiation strategies and practice self-advocacy. As a result, she is able to secure a job promotion and build stronger relationships with her colleagues.

In summary, developing interpersonal effectiveness skills can help neurodivergent individuals navigate social situations, build healthy relationships, and promote overall well-being. Through therapy or self-help techniques, individuals can learn to adapt these skills to their unique needs and preferences, leading to increased confidence and success in their personal and professional lives.

Chapter 7:Challenges neurodivergent individuals may face

While DBT can be a highly effective form of therapy for neurodivergent individuals, there are also common challenges that they may face when practicing DBT skills. Here are some of the most common challenges:

1. **Difficulty with emotional regulation**: Neurodivergent individuals may struggle with regulating their emotions due to their condition. This can make it difficult for them to practice DBT skills, such as mindfulness and distress tolerance, which require a certain level of emotional awareness and regulation.

2. **Sensory sensitivities**: Individuals with neurodivergent conditions such as autism spectrum disorder (ASD) and sensory processing disorder (SPD) may have sensory sensitivities that make it difficult to practice DBT skills, such as meditation or deep breathing. For example, certain sounds or smells may be overwhelming or distracting, making it difficult to focus on the skill.

3. **Executive functioning challenges**: Neurodivergent individuals may have challenges with executive functioning, such as planning, organizing, and prioritizing tasks. This can make it difficult to

practice DBT skills consistently, as they require a certain level of structure and routine.

4. **Communication difficulties**: Individuals with conditions such as ASD or ADHD may have difficulty with social communication, including expressing their needs and boundaries effectively. This can make it challenging to practice interpersonal effectiveness skills, such as assertiveness and effective communication.

5. **Cognitive inflexibility**: Neurodivergent individuals may struggle with cognitive flexibility, which refers to the ability to adapt to changing situations and perspectives. This can make it difficult to practice skills such as problem-solving and dialectical thinking, which require the ability to see multiple perspectives and consider different solutions.

Strategies for overcoming these challenges

Here are some strategies that can be helpful in overcoming the challenges that neurodivergent individuals may face when practicing DBT skills:

1. **Provide sensory accommodations**: Individuals with sensory sensitivities can benefit from sensory accommodations, such as noise-cancelling headphones or calming scents, to create a more comfortable and calming environment for practicing DBT skills.

2. **Break skills down into smaller steps**: Neurodivergent individuals may benefit from breaking DBT skills down into smaller steps and practicing them in a more gradual and structured way. This can help to build confidence and increase motivation to continue practicing the skills.

3. **Use visual aids**: Visual aids, such as diagrams or charts, can be helpful for neurodivergent individuals who struggle with executive functioning or processing verbal information. These aids can make the skills more concrete and easier to understand and remember.

4. **Incorporate technology-based tools**: Technology-based tools, such as meditation apps or mood tracking apps, can be helpful for neurodivergent individuals who struggle with traditional forms of mindfulness or emotion regulation. These tools can provide structure and support for practicing the skills in a more accessible way.

5. **Practice in a safe and supportive environment**: Creating a safe and supportive environment for practicing DBT skills can be helpful for neurodivergent individuals who struggle with communication difficulties or emotional regulation. This can include working with a trusted therapist or coach, practicing with a supportive group of peers, or practicing in a non-judgmental and accepting environment.

6. **Tailor the skills to individual needs**: DBT skills can be tailored to individual needs and preferences, taking into account the unique challenges and strengths of neurodivergent individuals. Working with a therapist or coach who has experience working with neurodivergent individuals can help to ensure that the skills are adapted in a way that is most helpful for the individual.

Despite these challenges, with appropriate adaptations and support, neurodivergent individuals can still benefit greatly from DBT skills. Some ways to adapt DBT skills for neurodivergent individuals include using visual aids, incorporating sensory accommodations, breaking down skills into smaller steps, and utilizing technology-based tools. It is also important to work with a therapist or coach who has experience working with neurodivergent individuals and can tailor the DBT skills to their specific needs and preferences.

Chapter 8: Putting it All Together

The goal of integrating the four modules of DBT into a comprehensive treatment plan is to create a holistic approach that addresses the unique challenges and capitalizes on the strengths of neurodivergent individuals. By combining mindfulness, interpersonal effectiveness, emotion regulation, and distress tolerance, this tailored approach ensures that all aspects of mental health and well-being are considered and addressed.

How to integrate the four modules of DBT into a comprehensive treatment plan:

Integrating the four modules of DBT involves developing a structured and consistent therapy schedule that incorporates each module. The treatment plan should be tailored to the individual's needs and goals, ensuring that each module is given adequate attention and time.

A typical DBT treatment plan may involve:

- Weekly individual therapy sessions focused on addressing specific challenges and working on targeted skills

- Weekly group skills training sessions, where individuals learn and practice DBT skills alongside peers

- Skills coaching, which provides support and guidance in applying skills to real-life situations

Throughout the treatment process, the therapist and individual work collaboratively to evaluate progress and make adjustments as needed.

Discussion of how to customize DBT for individual neurodivergent needs:

Customizing DBT for individual neurodivergent needs is crucial to ensure that the therapy effectively addresses the unique challenges and leverages the strengths of each person. This personalization process can make the therapeutic experience more engaging, relevant, and ultimately, more beneficial for neurodivergent individuals. Here are some key areas to consider when customizing DBT:

1. Sensory Sensitivities: Neurodivergent individuals may have heightened sensory sensitivities or unique sensory preferences. When customizing DBT, consider adapting mindfulness exercises or the therapy environment to accommodate these sensitivities, such as using soft lighting, offering noise-canceling headphones, or providing fidget tools.

2. Communication Styles: Neurodivergent individuals might have different communication styles or preferences. Customize therapy by using clear, concise language, incorporating visual aids, or using

alternative communication methods, such as written or visual cues, when needed.

3. Learning Styles: Each person has a unique learning style, which can affect their ability to absorb and retain information. Customize therapy by adjusting the pace or structure of sessions to match the individual's learning preferences, using repetition or reinforcement as necessary, and offering visual, auditory, or kinesthetic materials to support diverse learning styles.

4. Attention and Focus: Neurodivergent individuals may experience challenges with attention, focus, or executive functioning. Customize therapy by incorporating frequent breaks, setting short-term goals, and using engaging activities to maintain interest and focus during sessions.

5. Diagnosis-Specific Adaptations: Depending on the specific neurodivergent diagnosis, there may be additional adaptations necessary. For example, individuals with ASD may benefit from social stories, role-playing, or explicit instruction in social skills. Those with ADHD may require additional support in organization, time management, and impulse control. Tailor therapy to address the unique needs associated with each diagnosis.

6. Collaboration: Work collaboratively with the individual and, when appropriate, their family or

support network, to identify the most effective strategies for their unique needs. Encourage open communication and feedback to ensure that the therapeutic approach aligns with their preferences and goals.

7. Flexibility: Maintaining flexibility throughout the therapeutic process is key. As individuals progress, their needs or goals may change, and therapy should adapt accordingly. Regularly review and adjust the treatment plan to ensure it continues to meet the individual's evolving needs.

By customizing DBT for individual neurodivergent needs, therapists can create a supportive, engaging, and effective therapeutic experience that respects and celebrates the unique strengths and challenges of each person.

Overview of how to track progress and make adjustments to the treatment plan as needed:

Tracking progress and making adjustments to the treatment plan are essential components of DBT. This involves:

- Regularly reviewing the individual's progress in developing and applying DBT skills

- Discussing any challenges or obstacles encountered and brainstorming potential solutions

- Gathering feedback from the individual and, when appropriate, their family, about the effectiveness of the treatment plan

- Adjusting the focus or intensity of specific modules based on the individual's progress and needs

By continuously evaluating and adjusting the treatment plan, therapists can ensure that the individual receives the most effective and supportive care possible. This collaborative and dynamic approach to DBT fosters lasting change and growth for neurodivergent individuals, empowering them to live more fulfilling, resilient, and authentic lives.

Conclusion

In conclusion, DBT can be an incredibly beneficial form of therapy for neurodivergent individuals. By providing skills for emotional regulation, distress tolerance, mindfulness, interpersonal effectiveness, and emotion regulation, DBT can help neurodivergent individuals navigate social situations, manage overwhelming emotions, and promote overall well-being.

Some of the specific benefits of DBT for neurodivergent individuals include increased emotional awareness, improved communication skills, increased confidence in social situations, and decreased stress and anxiety. These benefits can lead to a higher quality of life and increased success in both personal and professional settings.

It is important to note that practicing DBT skills can be challenging, and neurodivergent individuals may face unique challenges when learning and implementing these skills. However, with the right adaptations and support, DBT can still be highly effective for neurodivergent individuals.

To encourage continued practice and support, it is important to seek out a therapist or coach who has experience working with neurodivergent individuals and who can tailor DBT skills to individual needs and preferences. It can also be helpful to connect with a support group or community of peers who are also practicing DBT skills.

In summary, DBT can be a powerful tool for neurodivergent individuals seeking to improve their emotional regulation, communication skills, and overall well-being. With continued practice and support, individuals can reap the benefits of DBT and live a more fulfilling and successful life.

Made in the USA
Columbia, SC
20 November 2023

26688301R00055